My Nanny Just Loves Cricket

by

Barry Clist

To Sarah,
Enjoy !!
Barry Clist
22/9/17.

Cover illustration by
Barry Clist

My Nanny Just Loves Cricket

Published by

Douglas Barry Publications

Kemp House
152 - 160 City Road
London
EC1V 2NX
ENGLAND

Tel 0870 879 3828
Fax 0870 879 2865
E-mail info@DouglasBarry.com
Web www.douglasbarry.com

FIRST PUBLISHED IN THE U.K. 2008

My Nanny Just Loves Cricket

COPYRIGHT 2008
©Douglas Barry Publications

All Rights Reserved. No part of this publication/document may be reproduced or transmitted in any form or by any means, electronic or mechanical, including photocopying, recording, or any information storage or retrieval system, without permission in writing of Douglas Barry Publications.
Written in 2008

British Library - A CIP Catalogue
record for this book is available
from the British Library.

I.S.B.N.   978-0-9553122-4-3

In memory of my Mother and Father who made my childhood such a precious time.

Acknowledgements

This book would not have been possible without Ellen, who so patiently listened and encouraged me, Sam and Greg, who made parenthood such fun and whose support I have always valued, and for the children I have taught who provided me with the inspiration for a number of these poems.

CONTENTS

	Page		Page
My Nanny Just Loves Cricket	14	The Mistake	44
Wishes	16	Dream	46
I Ain't Got No Bits	18	Conkers	48
Summer	20	Hiding Place	50
Secure	22	Mrs Dalton's Chair	52
If Pigs Could Fly	24	The Monkey	54
Kite	25	The Sparrows	58
Santa's Beard	26	Fox	62
The Impossible Poem	28	'Pass The Present'	66
Travelling By Car	30	Draw The Curtain	68
Release	31	Double Parked	70
Longitude and Latitude	31	Hands Up!	72
Treasures of Marble	32	Scared	74
Names	34	Having a Ball	76
Shore Crab	36	The Song	78
Explosion	38	What a Mess!	82
Have You Ever Wondered?	40	Smiles	83
Rooftop	42	Seat Number Eight	84

My Nanny Just Loves Cricket

My Nanny just loves cricket,
A gentlemanly game,
She sizes up the wicket
With her gentle lady frame.
She thrashes with her cricket bat
And belts a ball real hard,
She thumps it all around the place,
And is, by all, admired.

She wears cricketer's trousers,
All gleaming, snowy white,
And she's even been noticed
Playing late at night.
As the moon shines down upon her
She's been heard to say……..
"Four!" or "Six!" And "That's not out!"
Right through till break of day.

When I'm big I'll play like her,
I'll bowl a real mean ball
That'll shatter those three cricket stumps
That stand erect and tall.
But for now I'll watch my Nanny
And gather expertise,
I'll watch her bowling Yorkers
And scoring runs with ease.
She'll show me how to hold a bat
And how to bowl dead straight,
I know my Nanny is fantastic,
And I think she's really great!

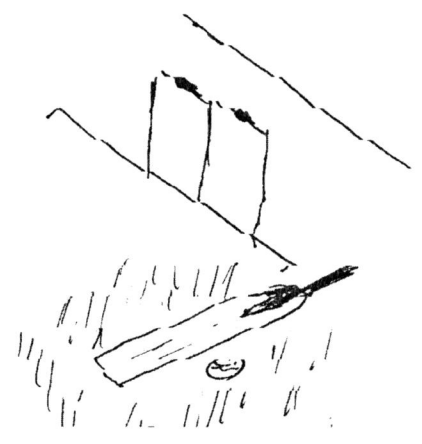

Wishes

Wishes are like bubbles,
They float around your head.
They glisten and they sparkle,
Let you have fun …………instead
Of thinking of your homework
And things you have to do,
Like all those horrid subjects
Which always worry you.

Now you can drive an engine
And you can search for gold.
You can fight great dragons,
Be a knight in days of old.

You can be a princess
Or a famous superstar.
You can be a tightrope walker
Or crash James Bond's new car.

You can score in the Cup Final,
Cheering crowds will shout your name,
But eventually you'll wake up
And you'll know it's just a game.

Because ………..
Wishes are just fantasy,
A game we like to play,
A way of chasing all the cares

Of this world right away.
But wait ! There may be wishes
That really can come true.
It depends on what you've wished for,
And if it's right for you.

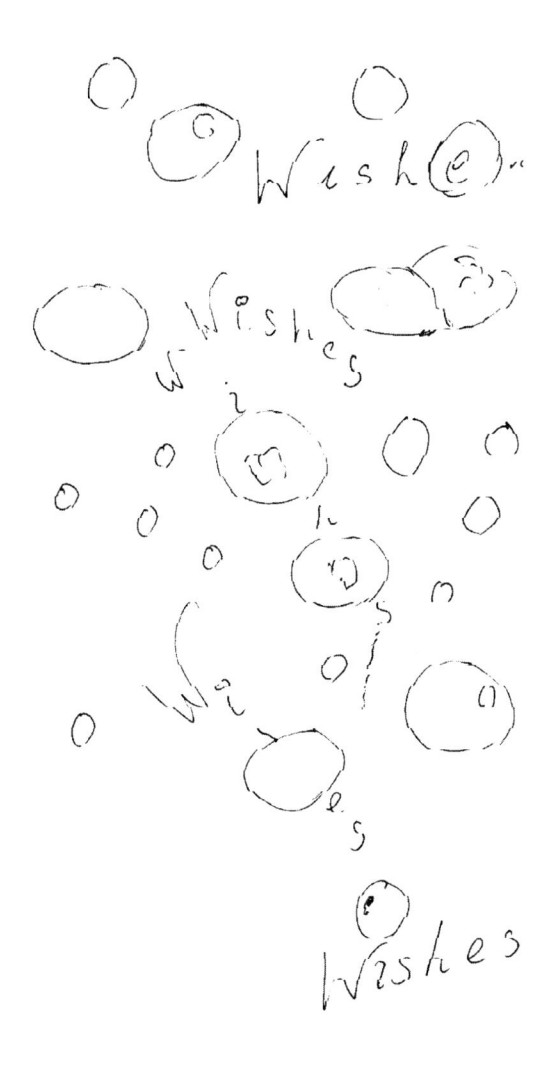

I Ain't Got No Bits

I'd like to build a sailing ship
That rides across the sea.
I'd like to watch it catch the wind,
With sails billowing free ....
But .. I ain't got no bits!

I'd like to build an aeroplane
That flies across the sky.
I'd like to watch it soar above
My head, as it flies high ....
But ..I ain't got no bits!

I'd like to build a huge robot
With hands as large as plates.
I'd like to watch it walk and talk,
And show it to my mates ....
But ..I ain't got no bits!

I'd like to do a big jig-saw
That spreads across the floor.
I'd like to do a bigger one
That stretches out the door ....
But ..I ain't got no bits!

These bits that I've got none of
Are causing me some grief.
I had them here the other day
But they were taken by a thief!

JIGSAW

Summer

Guns a 'blazing in the garden,
Bodies strewn on grassy lawn,
Children run in all directions,
Sweaty features, some forlorn.

Sunny days with games a plenty,
Swings and roundabout and slide.
Trees and countless bushy places
In and under which to hide.

These are days for all to savour,
Schools are closed and summer's come.
Sounds of laughter echo loudly
In the beaming, golden sun.

Then, at length, the evening quiet
Fills the place where once was noise,
Beds are filled with drowsy children
Worlds of dreams greet girls and boys.

Days are filled with great adventure,
Long days out and journeys home.
Summer's come and cares abandoned
Golden moments we've all known.

My Nanny Just Loves Cricket

Secure

Sticky ice pops,
Melting ice creams,
Things that you want
In your wildest dreams.
Greenest grass,
Coolest breeze,
Bermuda shorts,
Uncovered knees.

Picnic basket,
Clear blue sky,
Fizzy drinks,
Time rolling by.
Flight of swallows
Glide then dive,
Bees loud buzzing
Round their hive.

Summer days
When we're together,
Family
And Great Aunt Heather.
It is for all
A time of calm,
A time of safety
Free from harm.

23
My Nanny Just Loves Cricket

If Pigs Could Fly

If pigs could fly
We'd have a job
To get all of our bacon.
Maybe we would have a plate
Where rashers are forsaken,
Where eggs sit there in loneliness
And sausages aren't on.
If pigs could fly
That's what there'd be,
A breakfast almost gone!

Kite

Happy, flying, wind-spread kites,
Soar and dip from dizzy heights.
Pulled and tugged by girls and boys,
Swept by wind, they're nature's toys.
'Twas the children brought them here
From their homes (which are quite near),
But once released and free to soar
They are the children's toys no more.
Winds determine where they go
As children struggle on tip-toe
To hold and guide the swirling kite
From early morn to dead of night.

Santa's Beard

The child pulled back the curtain,
The street was gleaming white.
Santa must have trimmed his beard
And bits fell overnight.
They fell all over roadways
They fell all over grass
They fell all over rooftops
Where Santa's reindeer pass.

    He doesn't trim it often,
    In fact it's been some time,
    He hadn't trimmed it late last night
    At least not up till nine.
    Because, as he drew the curtain
    The streets looked pale and grey
    And as he woke this morning
    He expected it that way.

        But the child's face looked a picture
        As he stared upon the street,
        He rushed and found his clothing
        And pulled socks on both his feet.
        He scampered down the staircase
        Flung the front door open wide,
        Went back to get his wellies
        And then rushed right outside.

He turned and saw his footprints,
Deep, uniquely shaped.
He ran across and made some more
Pretending he'd escaped…………
Escaped a world of dullened grey
Where life's rich colours died
And entered a new kingdom
Where nothing dull survived.

He wishes Santa would trim his beard more often.
Do you ?

The Impossible Poem

Joanne sat back and wondered
Just what she should write
Looking out her bedroom window
Deep into the night.
She hated writing poetry
At any time of day
But to do it for her homework
Was insulting………… anyway

She sat there thinking …..

If I had a magic paintbrush
I would like to paint the sound
Of silver blades on frozen ice,
Snow falling all around.

If I had a magic orchestra
I would like to hear them play
The smell of ripened strawberries
Rainbow colours of the day.

If I went on a magic journey
And could travel anywhere,
I would go on through my wardrobe doors
To magic lands out there.

If I had a magic pencil
It could write the lines for me.
I would simply wish and there'd appear
My piece of poetry.

At length Joanna looked down again
At what she'd written now……..
Magic paintbrush ………..
Magic orchestra ……..
Magic journey ……….
Magic pencil ………
The words appeared somehow.
The poem that had seemed so hard
Was now, for her, complete.
She turned and smiled
She stretched and yawned
Then brushed her hair ………… quite neat.

She crept beneath her blanket
Where she could dream her dreams
Of magic days and magic nights
Where nothing's as it seems,
Where the word impossible
Has never once been said,
Where anything can happen
As you're snugly tucked in bed.

Travelling By Car

Concrete on the one side,
Plain grass on the other,
    Stuck inside this Maestro
    With my little brother.
        Whenever we're on journeys,
        Be they near or far,
            I wish my little brother
            Was in a different car.
        He is so aggravating,
        He never stops his chat,
    I simply want to shut him up
    Or hit him with a bat!
But I suppose I'm stuck, whatever,
    With my brother next to me,
I only hope we'll soon arrive
So I can be let free.

Release

I should have let my brain breathe,
My mother said to me,
So then she cut my hair quite short
And let my thought waves free.

Longitude and Latitude

Longitude
Is tall and long
From North to South
You can't go wrong
But latitude
Lies on its back
From West to East
It sets its track.

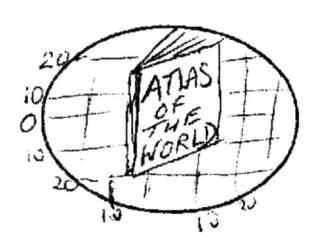

Treasures of Marble

Coffee colours,
Chocolate swirls,
Tiger stripes,
Battle unfurls.
Sapphire blues
Play great black knights,
Boys and girls
Have marble fights.
A duke, an earl,
An emperor gold,
Do battle royal
As of old.
Oilies, cats' eyes,
China pearls,
Great red devils,
Twisting curls.
Children combat
'Neath the sun,
The rain, the snow,
All weathers come.
But battle royal
Carries on
When twilight comes
And daylight's gone.

They play beneath
Electric light
Till one is vanquished
In the night.
At length
A victor does succeed
Like knight of old
On trusty steed.
With marble bag
And bulging treasure
It's booty great
Of boundless measure.

The one defeated will,
Once more,
Do battle royal
As before.
The victor proud
Salutes his foe
And together they
Decide to go.
They shake, they smile,
Day's battle done,
For after all
It was great fun.

Names

A note of explanation.
You may wonder why your parents chose the name they did for you. The names in this poem really are true. They have been collected from both Britain and the United States of America. After you have read this you may well be grateful that you were called by the name you have.

    The names used in this poem
    Aren't fictitious, they are true.
    You can sigh with deepest gratitude
    That none belong to you.

    How would you like
    The name Hazel May Call
    Or Della Short Speed
    Or Jack Waterfall?
    There are names in abundance
    I wouldn't like
    Such as Ima June Bugg
    And Thomas Might Strike,
    King Solomon Jones,
    Anna Dumpling Cheesecake,
    Nellie Hawk Eagle
    And George Harvest Bake.

As I read down the page,
Things became even worse,
Singular Onions Gallyhawks
And Carsin Reverse,
Susan Eatwell Burpitt,
Mary Hatt Box,
Strange Odor Andrews
And Jane Sometime Knox.

Parents can't be serious
Calling their child
Be Careful McGee
Or Anne Soften Wild.
It is true I assure you,
The evidence is clear
In this great list of names
I've discovered this year.

These names were collected
With assortment of facts,
Where some names have derived
From strange artefacts.
Names of plain objects,
Colours and shoes,
But my favourite and best
Was Strange Odor Andrews.

Shore Crab

I saw a decapod today
For the first time.
It had
One,
Two,
Three,
Four,
Five,
Six,
Seven,
Eight,
Nine,
Ten legs.
And none were like mine.

        Then I looked much closer
        And I saw another one,
        A crab in shallow water
        Beneath the noon day sun.
        Where there was one deca
        There now seemed to be two,
        A sort of double deca
        Staring back at you.

        Their bodies were quite knobbly,
        And they weren't that big in size,
        But they did look rather vicious
        With three teeth between their eyes,

I didn't go too near them,
Wasn't sure what they would eat,
And I didn't fancy losing
Either of my feet.
Anyway my Dad had said
"Be careful. Walk, don't run.
'Cause double deckers knock you down
And that isn't much fun."

I could have bent down, picked them up,
But I wasn't a fool.
So I left the little creatures
Sitting in their pool.

Explosion

I heard an explosion …….
In the playground …….
Just the other day.
An explosion of fists,
An explosion of words,
An explosion while I was at play.

I felt an explosion …….
In the playground …….
Just the other day.
An explosion of hate,
An explosion of fear,
An explosion while I was at play.

I saw an explosion …….
In the playground …….
Just the other day.
A bleeding nose,
A blackened eye,
An explosion of pain, of decay.

I wish there weren't explosions
In the playground …….
Any day.
No explosions of hurt,
No explosion of lies,
No explosions while I'm out at play.

My Nanny Just Loves Cricket

Have You Ever Wondered ?

Have you ever wondered
About things ?
Like …….
Why do we never see
Baby pigeons ?
Because I know there must be some.

Have you ever wondered
Why water
Doesn't wash away
Everything ?
Because it gets rid of sticky egg remains
From my plate,
And that's really tough!

Have you ever wondered
Why adults
Always seem
To stay
The same size?
Because they never get bigger
Even though
We've grown
And doubled our size
In just four years
At one school.

Have you ever wondered
Why most adults
Stop smiling
As soon as
They've forgotten
That they are really just big children ?

I have.

Rooftop

I stood on the rooftop
Of the old Norman church.
The clock chimed loudly
Every fifteen minutes,
Reminding me that time was passing.
I felt free
Up there.

I could see everything,
Even
Treetops on the hills,
Be it
Winter,
Summer,
Autumn,
Or spring.

I could see ....
Mrs Baker's garden,
Aunt Ethel's bungalow,
The gravel path that was to the side
And people down below.

I could hear …….
Dogs barking in the sheepy fields,
Distant traffic
Down the lane,
The rustle of the autumn leaves,
The patter
Of the rain.

        I could smell …….
        The scent of summer lavender,
        The warmth
        That filled the air.
        I could almost taste the freshness
        That was present
        Everywhere.

I loved to go there often,
As often as I'd please,
My father was the vicar
And he liked to feel the breeze.
Together we would stand there,
We would drink the scene right in,
And we would never tire of it,
No matter where we'd been.

        There was nowhere else I'd rather be
        Than up there with my Dad
        With my sheepy fields around me
        And the good times that we had …….
        Together.

The Mistake

Giggles started slowly,
Laughter followed on
As I walked into the playground
With my green school tee-shirt on.
It isn't that I'm wearing
Anything that's weird,
It's the haircut that I had last night
With which I now appeared.
You see, my hair was wavy,
A sort of shoulder length,
And I used to feel like Samson
With all his mighty strength.
But now I feel quite stupid,
And it's really not the same,
When a number of your classmates
Treat your head as just a game.
I hear their taunts already,
"Look at peanut! Here comes John."
They stood outside the grey school gate,
"And where's his hair all gone?"
I can put up with detentions,
I can put up with a lot
But to suffer like this, frankly,
Takes more than I have got.
So I think I'll ask my teacher
If she has a job or two,
Then I can stay indoors at break
Away from all of you.

"Now, what's this John ?" asked Mrs James,
(A headmistress stout and firm)
"You really shouldn't be here,
It's not the start of term.
We're not back till next Tuesday,
Here sharp at five to nine.
Go away. Enjoy yourself.
While the weather is still fine."
I walked back to the school gates,
My mates were still out there
Poking fun and shouting,
Making jokes about my hair.
I won't enjoy next Tuesday,
When I know my time has come,
As I step into the playground
And they start poking fun.

Dream

I'll dream of a place
Not far from here,
A place where there's peace,
Where no-one is near.
I'll dream of a place
Where I can go,
To be on my own,
And no-one will know
I am there.

        I'll dream of a time
        Not long from now,
        A time when there's calm,
        Then maybe …….somehow,
        I can dream of a time
        When I can be
        Alone ……. By myself
        And no-one will see
        I am there.

My Nanny Just Loves Cricket

Conkers

"Mine's a forty-niner."
"Mine's an eighty-three."
"Mine's a two – o – seven."
"Mine's infinity!"

"Mine's natural horse chestnut."
"Mine's toughened in the oven."
"Mine's been soaked in vinegar,
Like the other dozen."

Swinging strings,
Exploding seeds
Burst across the land.
For it is conker season
And battle has been planned.

Brother will fight brother,
Friend will seek out friend,
Whose conker will be conqueror
At the very end ?

All week the battle rages,
At playtime, lunch and tea.
Children with their conkers
Crashing constantly.

At length the season dies again,
Wars cease, peace comes once more,
And around the scars of battle
Lie scattered on the floor.

Some seeds survive to live again,
They grow horse chestnuts new,
And in time provide new conkers
For you …….
               And you …….
                             And you.

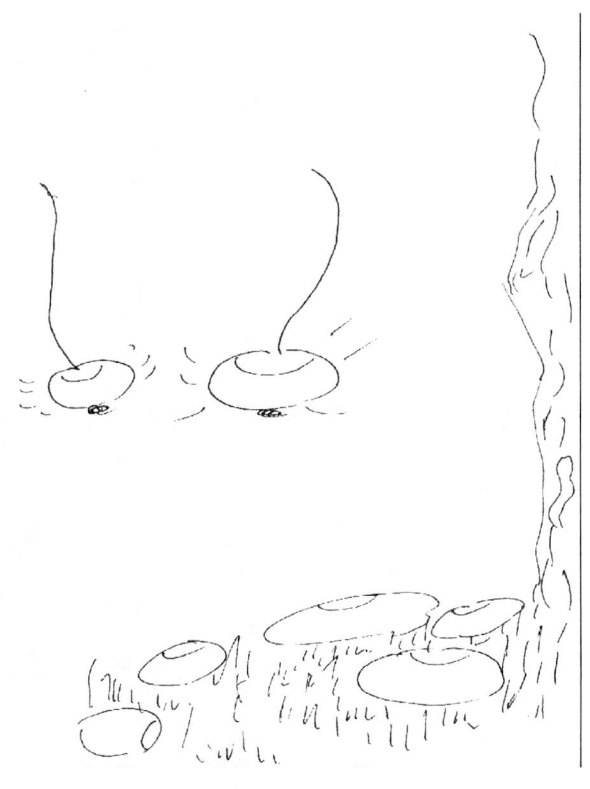

Hiding Place

My hiding place is very small,
It's my special kind of house.
In it I keep MY things,
MY valuables
And MY little pet mouse,
Derek.

I watch the squirrels dancing
High up in the trees.
They are so acrobatic
But they don't scrape their knees
Like I do.

Sometimes it is gloomy
In my secret place.
I can go for hours
And see no human face.
But I have my friends around me,
Below me
And above
And Mum's not here to tell me off
When I do the things I love.

I can leave my rubbish scattered
All over the floor,
Be as messy as I want to be
And not worry any more.
I can play among the undergrowth,
I can roll in grass and leaves,
I can stalk the wildlife with my bow
And swing among the trees.

I can chat to all the pigeons
That swoop outside my den.
I can talk to woodland creatures
And pay no heed to when
The time has come to leave this place
And go to my other home,
With badgers, hedgehogs, dormice,
Still out here free to roam.

It's not as if my parents
Mind me being here.
Because they both can see me,
As my house is really near.
I suppose that it is not so bad
Having them around,
You see if I get frightened
By any night time sound
I can climb down my rope ladder
And ask to go inside,
But otherwise I'll stay up here
Where only I can hide.

Mrs Dalton's Chair

My name is Archie Hatton
And I'm Mrs Dalton's chair.
I am always getting sat on
By her desk ……. I'm always there.
She says that I'm not comfy,
Tosses cushions on my seat,
Then she sits back and relaxes,
Stretches out her size ten feet.

I wish I were in her place
And my bottom was on her,
See how she'd like my wriggling
As the children called ME sir.
But I suppose that I am destined
To always be a seat,
And be crushed by Mrs Dalton
With her clumping size ten feet.

Ouch!

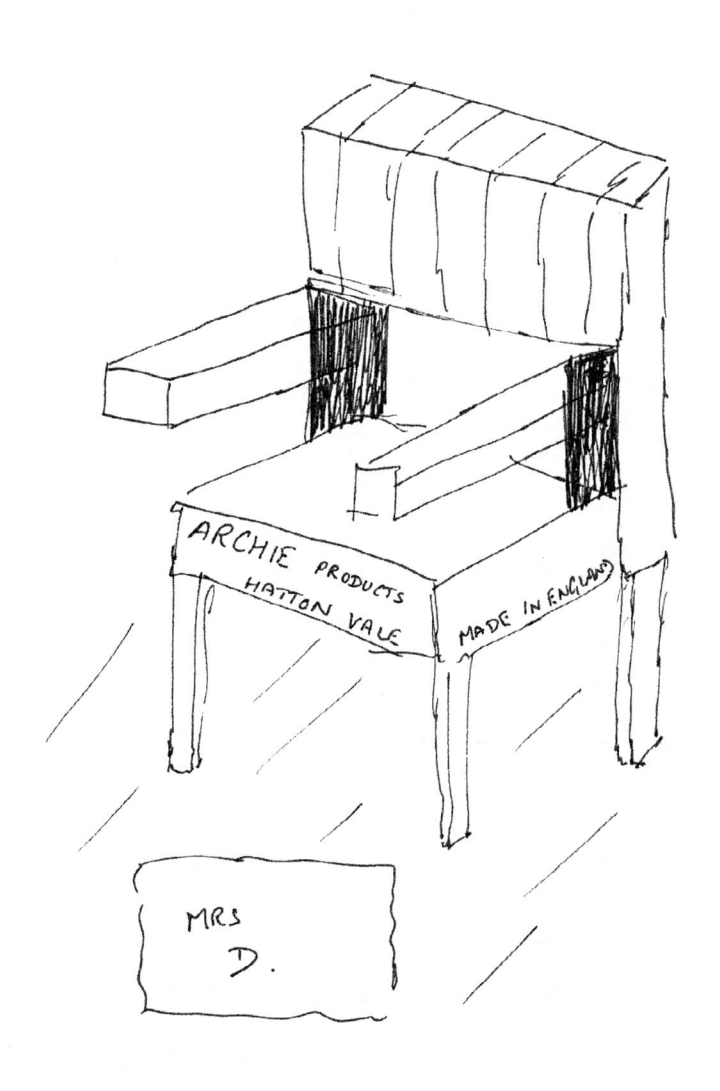

My Nanny Just Loves Cricket

The Monkey

Have you ever seen a monkey
Hanging upside down ?
Have you ever heard him saying
"Come and see my coat of brown ?
Come and join me in my jungle,
Come swing up high with me,
Come hang about, just for a while,
There's room up in this tree."

This monkey seemed quite different,
For his coat was not of skin,
Although he seemed to wear a coat
With monkey skin within.
The jacket he was wearing
Was made of thread and leather.
He seemed okay, I climbed the tree
And we went and swung together.

It really is quite strange, you know,
Looking down on people,
The sort of feeling steeplejacks
Get while on a steeple.
People look so different,
People look so small,
When you're up here in a tree top
High above them all.

The monkey was an acrobat,
An agile ape, no less,
Who swung among the tree tops
And, hazarding a guess,
We were heading to his hideout
High up in this tree,
He wouldn't stop his chattering
And tried to hurry me.

When we arrived together,
Exhausted, I fell down.
The monkey made himself at home,
Removed his coat of brown.
He opened up a wardrobe
And there, upon a rack
Were countless other jackets
To put upon his back.

I looked with awe and wonder
At the monkey's unique rail,
With its range of technicolours
Which could make your eyesight fail.
So many different textures,
So many varied shades,
So many up to date designs
And some with coloured braids.

The monkey turned and pointed
To the corner of the room,
There stood an antique sewing machine
Just beside a broom.
He sat down on a wooden chair
And then began to sew,
He made a bright red jacket
Quicker than you'd know.

The day went past so quickly,
And it had been so strange,
Well, have you ever seen a monkey
Who makes a fashion range ?
He hung up his last creation
And led me to the door,
"Come let's enjoy the weather
And swing about some more."

We swung and swung and swung again,
Until it was quite late,
And then we swung a little more,
In fact, till half past eight.
Then suddenly I realised
That having swung for hours
My Mum was calling out my name
Somewhere among the flowers.

I called out "Mum, I'm way up here!"
"Come down to me, my lad.
I'm really going to tell you off
Because you've been so bad."
I looked around for help now
But the monkey'd disappeared
So I swung down very carefully,
To meet the Mum I feared.

It was worth the telling off she gave me
For being out so late,
And she wouldn't hear excuses
That I'd been out with a primate.
She just said that I was grounded,
I suppose quite literally,
And I feel that it will be some time
Before she lets me near a tree.

The Sparrows

There are just seven trees
Outside our flats
Which are used by squirrels,
Birds and cats.

It's the one on the end
Which fascinates me,
With it's tall shiny bark
That looks silvery.
From high in its branches
I keep hearing a sound,
Like baby birds calling
For food to be found.

I think they are there,
I can just hear their call,
When all around's quiet,
With no sound at all.

"I wish we could see it,"
Said Darren one day,
"But we can't go up there,
It's too far away."
But Millie Warrender,
Who had much more nous,
Said we could see it
If we came round to her house.

"Don't be so daft,"
Came Darren's reply,
For he was indignant,
"It's up way too high!"
"No, you great dumb-bell,
My home's way up there,
On the fourth floor above us,
We can go by the stairs.
Then from above
We'll be able to see
What's inside the nest
That's up in this tree."

We raced up the staircases
One after the other,
When we reached the top
We saw Millie's brother.

All of us looked
At the nest, now below,
Me, Millie and Darren,
And John, in a row.
There were five baby sparrows,
"They're hungry," said John,
"It'll be just two weeks
Then they'll fly and be gone.
You know, sparrows build nests
Where holes can be found,
In thatch, walls and hedges,
And places around.

These sparrows took care
Not to be seen,
Their nest's in a hole
Where wood had once been."

We all stood and marvelled
At John's words, so wise,
He was just eight years old
And, to me, a surprise,
That someone so small
Should have knowledge like this.
He knew so much more
Than me or his sis.

Professors of science
Could not have explained
The great deal of knowledge
And wisdom I'd gained.

Darren and me,
Well, we had to go.
We picked up our bags
And moved off, rather slow.
John just looked on,
And then, with a smile,
Said he'd have to go in
As well, for a while.

There are just seven trees
Outside our flats
Which are used by squirrels,
Birds and cats.

It's the one on the end,
Which fascinates me,
With it's tall, shiny bark,
That looks silvery,
Because high in its branches,
Way up, off the ground,
Is a world that we missed
But now we have found.

I know it is there
I hear sparrows call,
When all around's quiet
With no sound at all.

Fox

The teacher glanced up,
His face, kind.
"I wrote this poem
Myself.
Try to see,
Try to imagine,
How this animal feels."

'Dawn breaks
Across the frosty hill top.
The countryside
Lies bleak and empty.
Near the young ash
Stands the fox,
Surveying the line of prints
He has left behind,
Breaking the whitish crust
Of the landscape.
The tracks tell the story
Of the night.
Only the trail of an eager vole
Shares the scene,
Disappearing down a hole nearby,
A tunnel it had dug so eagerly
For its own survival.'

"Please Sir, can you tell me,
Is it really true,
That foxes, when they're hungry,
Come chasing after you?
Because in this book I read, Sir,
It said, at dead of night,
(Especially in Winter,
When the snow is whitest white),
That foxes come right into town
In search of food to eat,
And I'm really worried now, Sir,
Because I'm made up of meat."

"Do not worry, Alexander,
They won't come after you,
They could come into town though,
That much is often true.
For foxes, deep in Winter,
Find food is hard to get,
But in town, where it's all slushy,
(And your feet get rather wet),
Foxes come at dead of night
And look around for scraps,
Find holes in garden fences,
Or any bigger gaps.
They sniff around your rubbish,
Their sense of smell's acute,
Tear open bags quite ruthlessly
And carry off their loot.

For they have hungry mouths to feed,
Just like your family,
And they don't have hot dinners
Served up so readily."

"I feel sorry for the fox, Sir,
During winter's cold.
It can't be easy eating,
Food that's stale or old.
But thank you, Sir, for telling us,
I must have seemed a fool,
Though I must admit I worried
Quite a lot about it all.
Now that you've explained it,
It will help me understand
'bout foxes and small animals
That roam across our land."

My Nanny Just Loves Cricket

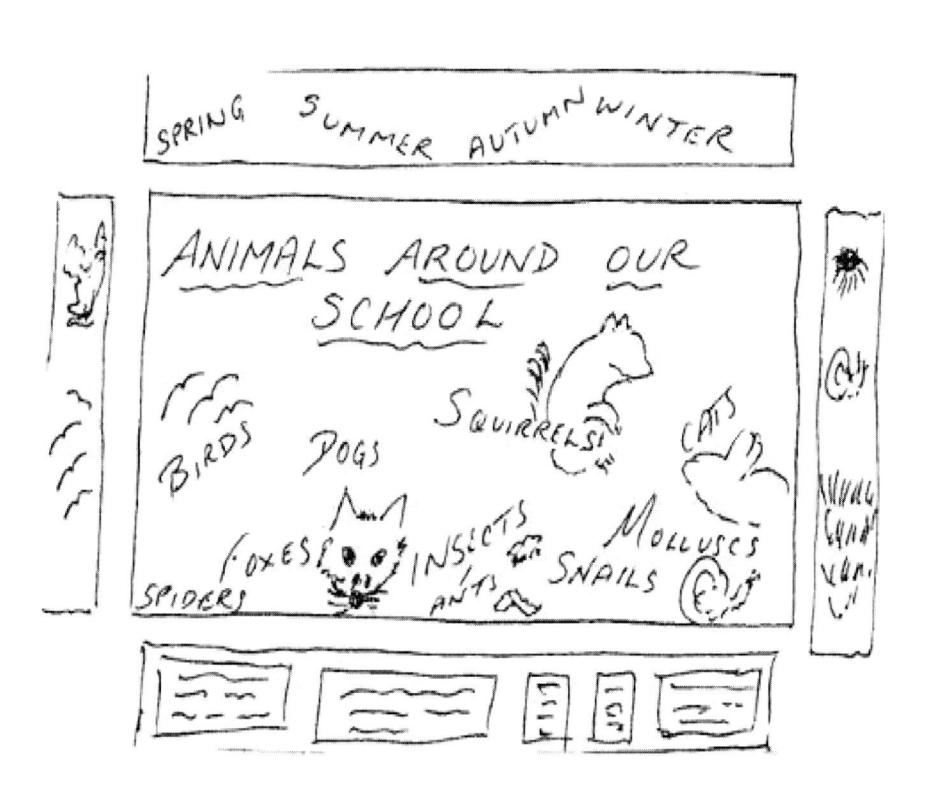

'Pass The Present'

I was bought this woolly jumper
From my Auntie Clarabelle,
It had sixteen different colours
And some pockets on as well.
I tried it on this morning,
But it really didn't fit
It could have fitted Dad though
So I've given him it! (wrapped of course!)

I was bought this pile of soapy stuff
With things that make baths bubble,
The problem is that I don't like
To wash it's so much trouble.
So I've wrapped it up a second time
And left it near the tree
With a label which now simply reads,
'With love for you, Mummy.'

Then there's these hankies from my Grandad,
But his eyes they're not too grand
Because they're covered in pink flowers
Now don't misunderstand
'Cause <u>even</u> <u>I</u> use hankies
When my nose is wet and runny,
But I've rewrapped them for my sister
And I saved myself some money.

There's this pair of brand new trainers
From my mother's sister, Mabel
But I'm size three and these are ones
And you should have seen the label.
Made in Taiwan by 'Twinkletoes'
In letters clear and tall
So I've rewrapped them for my brother
Because he can't read at all!

On each and every Christmas Day
I'm the first to wake and rise.
I unwrap my presents eagerly
Before the sun lights up the skies,
And I never do my shopping
For presents till that day
Because most of what I'm given
I can simply give away.

Lastly, just a word of thanks to Cyril,
He's my dad's pal down the street
He couldn't think of what to get
And I think that's really neat.
Now all he sent me was an envelope
Quite unlike everyone
And in it was a ten pound note
With a card which said, 'Have Fun!'

Draw The Curtain

"Go get a pencil"

Teacher said

And then go draw the curtains.

So I went and pulled them

Tightly shut

And darkness fell for certain.

"I can't see!"

I cried in vain

"Don't worry!" said my teacher

"We won't do art

We'll watch a film

An exciting double feature."

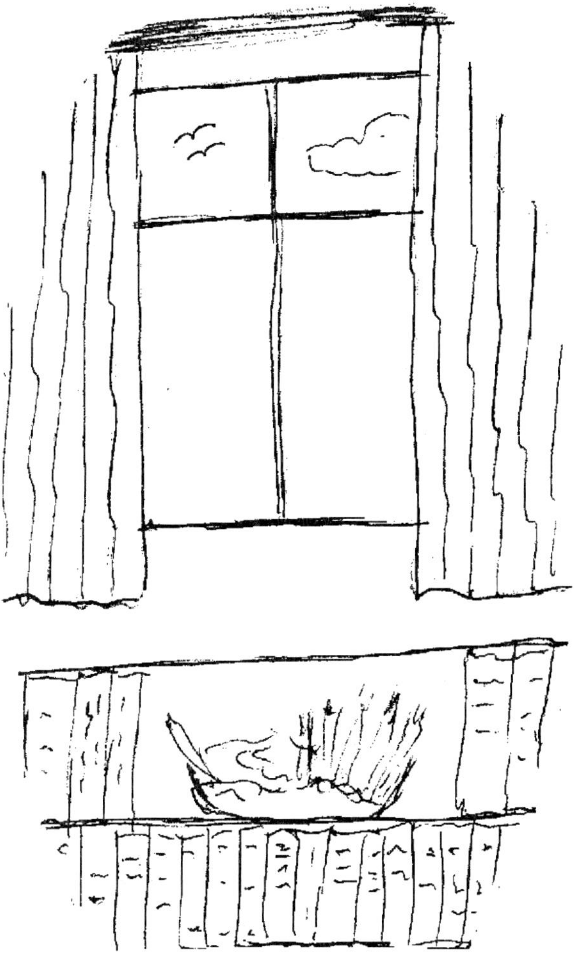

Double Parked

Santa rolled about a bit
In my garden full of snow,
Dad noticed him and had a word
And told him he should go.
Santa stood and brushed himself,
And as the snowflakes fell about
He said he couldn't go that far
His reindeer were worn out.
He showed us them, parked in the kerb
On double yellow lines
With tickets in their antlers
And endless other fines.
He said that they were hungry,
That their energy had gone,
But could it be that we could help
Santa's reindeer to go on ?

We went into the kitchen
And mixed all sorts of stuff,
We whisked and stirred and whisked again
Until we had enough.
Before us was a potion
Which sparkled like the stars,
With cereals and chocolate drops
And sliced up bits of Mars.
We fed it to the reindeer
Who ate it greedily
Their strength returned and Santa smiled
And jumped back in with glee.

He thanked us both and waved a wave
Which filled us with delight,
He wished us Merry Christmas
And flew off into the night.

Hands Up!

I have raised my hand so many times
During school assembly.
To try and answer questions
In a manner, keen and friendly.
But no one ever notices
Or if they do, they just pass by,
It is pretty obvious to me
I'll just have to catch their eye.

Now I'm raising my arm straight up,
I could flap it like a bird,
I could wave it really quickly,
I know it sounds absurd.
But I want to answer questions,
I am keen and I'm alert
My arm's been in the air so long
It really starts to hurt!

So ….. I'll try the new one fingered wiggle,
Or the one with puffed out chest,
There's the two arm straight surrender
That's the one I like the best,
Because it's obviously no good
Just raising my right arm,
I'll have to use initiative,
Great cunning …. even charm.

I will smile ever so sweetly,
I will sit up straight and tall,
I'll make sure I'm not distracted
By the pictures on the wall.
Yes .. they'll certainly not miss ME
With my new response technique
With my range of arm positions
They will have to let me speak …..

Sometime!

Scared

Have you ever been scared
And wanted to hide ?
Have you felt insecure
Or endlessly cried ?
Have you ever had worms
And great stringy snakes
Stuck in your stomach
When you've made mistakes ?
Did your heart beat faster ?
Did your body just shake ?
Was your head simply spinning ?
Did your willpower break ?
All of these feelings
Crowd in on me
When I'm frightened, feel helpless,
And long to be free.
When I'm scared or feel trapped
And I can't get away
When I feel insecure
Like I do today
I just try to escape
But there's nowhere to go
And the worms and the snakes
Just continue to grow.

My Nanny Just Loves Cricket

Having a Ball !

Flat ball,
   Long ball,
      Aerial ball,
         Square ball,
            Short ball,
               High ball,
                  Dead ball,
                     Cannon ball.
                        Goalie's ball,
                           Defender's ball,
                            Lobbed ball,
                              Chipped ball,
                                Dropped ball,
                                  Corner ball,
                                  Loose ball,
                                       Hand ball !
                                 Poor ball,
                               Wasted ball,
                             Easy ball,
                          Good ball,
                       Rolling ball,
                   Lucky ball,
                   Deflected ball,
                 Cross ball.
              Bouncing ball,
           Your ball !
        My ball !
      Runaway ball !
No ball !

My Nanny Just Loves Cricket

The Song

My Mum shouted at me.
I didn't know why.
She shouted again
And I started to cry.
She went on and on
About this thing and that,
So I sat down and cuddled, Wilfred,
My cat.

He might explain
What I had done bad,
I hadn't known then
But I sure wish I had.
Most of my life
My Mum is just fine,
But I hate my Mum shouting
At me, anytime.

On this one occasion,
I was singing, that's true,
A real funny song
That I'd learnt from Jack Blue.
It had some strange words
That I didn't quite know,
And I'd been told once before
That they'd have to go.

I sung it real quiet
As I cleaned my teeth,
Upstairs, in the bathroom,
With sink underneath,
And it's not as if the toothpaste
Is that hard to clean
Off tiles and off mirrors
And places it's been.

But my Mum, she was furious,
Sent me to my room.
I heard water running
And knew that quite soon
She'd clean every surface,
Remove every stain,
She'd then come along
To see me again.

I let Wilfred go,
I felt that was right
As she sat down beside me
On that summer's night.
She explained that the language
I'd used in that song
Was unnecessary
And utterly wrong.
She said that my singing,
With a mouthful of paste,
Wasn't quite the done thing
And caused her distaste.

My Nanny Just Loves Cricket

Now, as for my friend,
Or, so called, Jack Blue,
I went back and told him
Our friendship was through.
I told him the story
And HE was upset,
He seemed really sorry
And his eyes were all wet.
I learnt that new song
From Emily's brother,
And what's even worse,
He taught me another.
I went home last night,
Sung them to my Dad
And he shouted at ME
For being so bad.

We both decided
To avoid Emily's brother,
And if he came up
To sing yet another,
We'd tell him our feelings
Or just walk away,
Like our Mums and Dads told us
Just yesterday.

I'm now much more careful
With songs that I choose,
And far more selective
With words that I use.

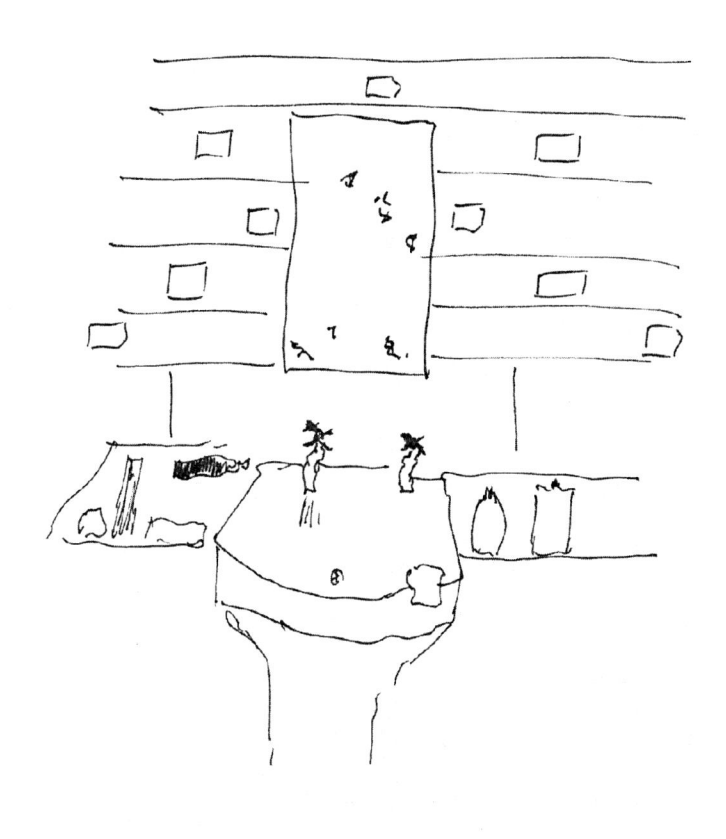

My Nanny Just Loves Cricket

What a Mess!

Lessons used to be exciting
As we'd explore with glee,
Those things, which in discussion,
We'd examine naturally.
But now we can't diversify
Transform, deflect, digress
As we'll affect curriculum
And leave it in a mess.

Smiles

My Mum says,
"Smiles make the day better,
Make the sun brighter,
Make the trees greener,
And make the flowers more colourful."

      My Dad says,
      "Smiles make the world go round,
      Make our home a happier place,
      Make music sound sweeter,
      And help to keep the peace."

Mr Davis, 6D's Teacher says,
"Smile, enjoy your work,
It will help you get on better.
Never be afraid to ask,
We all need help sometimes."

      My Teacher says,
      "Sit down !" grumpily.
      "Go out quietly!"
      "Don't ask silly questions!"
      And, "Don't make a fuss!"

She never smiles……………
I don't know why.

      But I wish she did!

Seat Number Eight

"Katy sit in seven,
Steven, you're in eight,
Simon, in eleven,
Molly .. you just wait."

This can't be right
Please move me miss!
I can't sit here
It's prejudice!

She's a girl
And I'm a boy
My confidence
You'll just destroy!

Can't I sit there
With Billy Flynn?
There's an open space
Right next to him.

"That is my seat
Young Master Brown
Yours is eight
So just sit down!"

I knew that then
I must relent
And sit myself
With Katy Brent.

I huffed and puffed
And wheezed and sighed
As my pleas to move
Had been denied.

But the journey
Wasn't all that bad
As Katy smiled,
Shared sweets she had.

We talked a bit
About our roads
And Mums and Dads
And frogs and toads.

And then I found out
SHE WAS COOL
'Cos she supported
Liverpool!

We talked and talked
And talked some more
Till we saw Miss Barnes
By the front coach door.

"Time to get off.
Just wait outside
And wear your uniform
With pride.

Behave yourselves,
All be polite,
Enjoy your day,
But stay in sight!

Line up in twos
And wait for us
Helpers first,
Then, leave the bus.

I missed Katy
As we walked around
And we explored
The castle grounds.

On the way back
I hope I'll be
By Katy's side,
Just her and me.

She's now a friend,
A first class mate.
On our return
I'll grab seat eight.

As long as she's in seven …
Of course!